2

ALPHONSE

by
WAJDI MOUAWAD

translated
by
Shelley Tepperman

Alphonse

or the adventures of Pierre-Paul-René,
a gentle boy with a one-note voice who was
never surprised by anything

Wajdi Mouawad

Translated by
Shelley Tepperman

Playwrights Canada Press
Toronto • Canada

Playwrights Canada Press
54 Wolseley St., 2nd fl. Toronto, Ontario CANADA M5T 1A5
416-703-0013   fax 416-703-0059
orders@playwrightscanada.com • www.playwrightscanada.com

Playwrights Canada Press acknowledges the support of the taxpayers of Canada and the province of Ontario through The Canada Council for the Arts and the Ontario Arts Council.

Cover art by Lino. Production Editor: Jodi Armstrong

National Library of Canada Cataloguing in Publication

Mouawad, Wajdi, 1968-
[Alphonse. English]
    Alphonse / Wajdi Mouawad ; translated by Shelley Tepperman.

Translation of: Alphonse, ou, Les aventures extraordinaires de Pierre-Paul-René, un enfant doux, monocorde et qui ne s'étonne jamais de rien.
A play.
ISBN 0-88754-632-3

    I. Tepperman, Shelley II. Title. III. Title: Alphonse. English.

PS8576.O87A7613 2002   jC842'.54   C2002-904798-6
PQ3919.2.M665A7613 2002

First edition: October 2002.
Printed and bound by AGMV Marquis at Quebec, Canada.

Translator's Dedication:

For Alon Nashman

For the Tepperman boys: Paul, Adam, Joey and Jacob

PLAYWRIGHT'S NOTE

Alphonse never would never have been written if it hadn't been for the program "Fragment" produced by François Ismert at Radio Canada FM in 1992, a year of grace. "Fragment" was a veritable beacon for all those who yearned to tell stories. It was within the context of that program, a true hazy landscape of the imaginary, that the characters of Alphonse, Walter, the Wild Child, Judith and the Cave were born.

If this text could serve as a reminder of "Fragment," justice will have been done.

—Wajdi Mouawad

NOTE ON THE TRANSLATION

A previous English translation of *Alphonse*, based on an abridged version of the play adapted for their production, was commissioned in 1994 by Théâtre de l'Arrière-scène. It was workshopped at Playwrights' Workshop Montreal in 1995 with actor Chris Heyerdahl and Peter Smith as dramaturg.

That earlier English version was read in Vancouver at "Acts of Passion", a showcase of Québécois plays produced by Ruby Slippers and Pink Ink Theatres. It was subsequently premiered by Pink Ink Theatre at Vancouver's Firehall Arts Centre in 1998. Mike Stack performed under Sandhano Schultz's direction. Nicole Dextras and Del Surjik designed set and costumes respectively, and Andreas Kahre designed the soundscape.

This book contains a brand new translation of the full published text of *Alphonse*, commissioned by Lynda Hill and Theatre Direct Canada. It was workshopped in Montreal in June, 2002 with Lynda Hill and Alon Nashman. At that time, cuts and modifications to the published French text were made by the author or with the author's approval. This new translation contains characters and episodes that had been cut for the abridged version. Their inclusion brings a profoundly spiritual dimension to the piece.

Thanks to the Writing and Publication Section of the Canada Council for the Arts, Soraya Peerbaye, Peter Hinton, Serge Marois, Chris Heyerdahl, Peter Smith, Elaine Kennedy, and all those who offered comments and feedback on the first translation so many years ago. And thanks especially to Lynda Hill, the motor behind this re-visioned translation, for her passion and commitment.
—Shelley Tepperman

This version of *Alphonse* was commissioned by Theatre Direct Canada in 2001, and premiered at DuMaurier Theatre, Harbourfront Centre, Toronto in November 2002 with the following company:

ALPHONSE   Alon Nashman

Artistic Director, Theatre Direct Canada: Lynda Hill
Directed by Lynda Hill and Alon Nashman
Set and Costumes designed by Vikki Anderson
Lighting designed by Michael Kruse
Original Music and Sound design: Cathy Nosaty
Stage Management by Tamerrah Chiyoko Volkovksis

Theatre Direct Canada would like to acknowledge Theaturtle and Artistic Director Alon Nashman who produced the Toronto premiere at the Toronto Fringe Festival in 2000.

— —●— —●— —

The original French version *Alphonse* was first produced in Beloeil, Quebec on December 12, 1993 by the Théâtre de l'Arrière-scène. It was directed by Serge Marois with a set by Paul Livernois assisted by Pierre Tremblay. Lighting was by Claude Cournoyer, costumes were by Georges Lévesque and music was by Pierre Labbé. *Alphonse* was performed by the author, Wajdi Mouawad, who is also an actor. The actor Emmanuel Bilodeau also performed the play occasionally.

A staged reading had previously taken place at the restaurant/ theatre La Licorne, directed by Alexis Martin, on Tuesday, April 6, 1993, as part of the 7th edition of the Semaine de la dramaturgie québécoise.

Since 1993 Wajdi Mouawad has performed *Alphonse* more than one hundred times, in Canada and in Europe.

ALPHONSE
•••••••••••••••

VOICE IN THE DARK
———•———•———•———

When we're little,
No one tells us very much.
So we imagine.
Later,
Imagining gets kind of complicated.
So we ask for information.
And so we become grownups and there's nothing wrong with
     that.
It's the natural order of things.
And things are well-designed
Because they prevent us from going backwards
Which is a very good thing.
And things are well-designed
Because they prevent us from going backwards
Which is a very good thing.
Because,
If by some impossible twist of fate,
A man crossed paths with the child he used to be, and they
     both recognized each other, they would both crumple to
     the ground, the man in despair, the child in terror.

ALPHONSE'S FAMILY
——•——•——•——

I have a little brother.

His name's Alphonse.

He's a brave kid, Alphonse: his green eyes look right at you.
When he walks down the street, people don't notice him.
He doesn't want anyone to notice him. Anyway, he's just
not the kind of kid people notice.

Tonight Alphonse didn't come home from school. My mother's
sitting in the living room, her knitting beside her.

My father's smoking by the wide-open window staring into the
night,

my sister's asleep (actually, she's just pretending)

and me, I'm sitting in the kitchen, worrying about Alphonse.
Where the hell can he be? The little weasel.

Something must have happened or he would have called! the
mother exclaimed from the living room. The father turned
and spit in her face to shut her up.

The father had already thrown in the towel. It's understand-
able, he was too upset.

After working like a dog my whole life, sweating away my
youth, sweating away my good looks, my elegance, all for
my family.

And what a family!

An ugly wife who knits non-stop, a daughter who still isn't
married and who nobody wants,

and an ungrateful son who just stands there in front of me
smirking superciliously.

And the last one, the youngest,

Alphonse,

the one I'd put all my hopes in,

now he's gone. No-one knows where.

What have I done with my life? Why didn't I listen to myself
back then "You aren't made to have a family" and now look
what's happened! Your youngest son's just disappeared!
I don't blame him, I'd have done the same thing!

Actually, Alphonse was walking along a country road but we're not supposed to know that just yet.

I really love Alphonse. He listens to me when I speak, and when I need help he's always there. Where is he? Life has given me nothing: my daughter's crying into her pillow, my son, the eldest one, must be reading in the kitchen (that one doesn't give a damn about anything!) and my husband who used to be so handsome, a man now all alone in life, a man who used to be so strong, has to steady himself on the door frame so he doesn't fall. My Goodness! They say it's going to be cold tomorrow. And Alphonse didn't take his sweater with him! I mustn't forget to buy cheese for tomorrow.
We mustn't scold Alphonse. We'll have to try and understand why he left. That's it.

In her bed, the sister started to cry. She had said one or two prayers but what good was that? Alphonse won't be coming back. She was used to looking after him. When he was little she took him for walks, she bathed him, she gave him little presents. He was her baby brother. At night, when Alphonse would awaken, she'd wake up right away too, stirred by a feeling of protectiveness.
Alphonse, where are you going? I'd ask him every time.
I'm going to get a glass of water.
Do you want me to get it for you?
No thanks, sis, I need to stretch my legs.
He always said exactly the same thing: it was to stretch his legs!
But I know it was really to sneak into the pantry and stuff his face with marshmallow cookies.

Actually, the real reason Alphonse would get up was very very different...

THE REAL REASON
ALPHONSE WOULD GET UP
IN THE MIDDLE OF THE NIGHT
——•——•——•——

Alphonse would get up each night to meet—in the hallway
that led to the kitchen—Pierre-Paul-René, a gentle boy
with a one-note voice who was never surprised by anything, and who only he, Alphonse, was acquainted with. In
the time it took to go from the bedroom to the kitchen,
Alphonse and Pierre-Paul-René could live out a thousand
adventures in the dark.

Pierre-Paul-René always appeared to him at night since it was
during a ferocious stormy night when Alphonse had gotten
up to get a glass of water that they met for the first time.

On that unforgettable night Alphonse had found himself sitting up in his bed, his eyes wide open; the surrounding
darkness stuck its tongue out at him.
In the next bed his brother was fast asleep and seemed totally
consumed by mysterious affairs no-one else had access to.
The closed shutters painted the room a thick jelly-black. The
storm was magnificent. Alphonse was very thirsty. The
kitchen was far away. Very far away. Between the kitchen
and Alphonse lay the hallway, and in the hallway anything
could happen. Because first, Alphonse had to go all the
way down the hallway to reach the switch that would fill it
with light. The hallway. That cold hallway that led to a
bottomless living room and a dining room that loudly
digested creaky wood. Alphonse's pyjamas were too big,
too long. Getting out of bed seemed unthinkable under
such conditions. But he was so thirsty and the water would
be so nice and cool in the earthenware jug.
His brother rolled over. Waking him up would unquestionably
jeopardize his internal affairs.

The hallway furrowed its eyebrows at him. Alphonse was
terrorized! And he knew very well that he couldn't even
consider waking up his mother. Because she was certain to

get angry and that would be awful. Really, Alphonse, you're not a little boy anymore was what she said to him the last time. But now the horrible thirst ravaging his throat was so unbearable it made him forget his fear for an instant and coaxed him out of bed. By the time he reached the edge of the hallway, it was too late to turn back! The storm kept on crashing louder and louder, and in a flash of lightning the hallway filled with sordid characters lurking at the foot of the wall... the floor was nonexistent, and falling into the void seemed inevitable. And then! Right then, in a flash of lightning, Alphonse saw, at the other end of the hallway—for just a brief moment—a boy looking right at him.

"Alphonse! he thought he heard in the middle of the storm.

—Who are you?

—I'm Pierre-Paul-René! A gentle boy with a one-note voice and I'm never surprised by anything. I've come to live inside your head, Alphonse. From now on you won't be afraid when you get up in the middle of the night and unafraid you'll cross the hallway to get your glass of water because I will always be there."

And that was it!

That night, when he went back to bed, Alphonse dreamed about Pierre-Paul-René... strange dreams, very strange dreams...

Pierre-Paul-René was sitting at the foot of a building. Children played serenely in the shade of some brontosauri frolicking gaily in the grass. The wind gusted through the falling rain. Pierre-Paul-René was happy. Little by little, the rain died down and the wind took a bow, having chased away the clouds. The daylight dissolved into silence, the children had disappeared, and the brontosauri were levitating. Suddenly, sucked up by a giant vacuum cleaner that appeared out of a cottonosity of clouds, Pierre-Paul-René found himself inside a tube that smelled like seashells and sausages and which was pulling him along at an incredible speed. Pierre-Paul-René thought it was the end of the world and therefore decided it would be pointless to scream, since he was a gentle boy with a one-note voice and was never surprised by anything. He remained absolutely calm and let himself be dragged through the dark when he felt himself slow down and land on a wooden floor. There were five nightlights that lit up nothing but Darkness, that fallen Princess famous for frightening children. Pierre-Paul-René decided to play it safe. He called out: "Yo, is anybody there?

—Yes there's somebody, came the reply. There's Sabayon the Fourth, your king, and I've chosen you for a mission!

—Why me?

—Because you're the only child left.

Sabayon the Fourth continued: Yes, this mission is crucial, Pierre-Paul-René, to bring back the children of our country, because there are no more cakes, the pastry chefs have all disappeared, some dead, others eaten by the enemy and the rest turned into popcorn!"

Pierre-Paul-René, who's a gentle boy with a one-note voice who's never surprised by anything, was nonetheless a bit surprised.

"No more cakes? he said.

—No!

—Drat!

—What is the world coming to? People don't believe in miracles anymore. The pastry chefs have disappeared! The situation is critical. Pierre-Paul-René, you must go to Pastryburg, that savage land teeming with legends and traps. There you must find the cake recipes the pastry chefs took with them and bring them back here. Go, Pierre-Paul-René, you must go to Pastryburg. Go. You must also beware of the infamous Flupan, the prince of excessively gluttonous gluttons. Go, Pierre-Paul-René, go, go, go, I tell you, you must go to Pastryburg, go–

—OK, OK, I get the message.

—Go, run, fly, don't forget the children, and remember me!"

Then Sabayon the Fourth opened the great vacuum cleaner that was his body and Pierre-Paul-René walked out. The landscape around him was extremely indecisive. The sky kept changing from white to blue and back again; the trees, not knowing what season it was, kept losing their leaves but new ones would sprout immediately; the sea turned to desert and the desert turned to wind which multiplied among the stalks of the flowers, which were frantically opening and closing. Faced with so much indecision, Pierre-Paul-René was overwhelmed. He didn't know which foot to put forward first to begin his journey, and he didn't know what direction to take either.

I have to make a decision, he thought.

ALPHONSE'S FAMILY NOTIFIES THE POLICE

The brother, still in the kitchen, kept silently repeating to himself that yes, something might have happened to Alphonse, and that would be awful. And if he'd been kidnapped, taken prisoner; yes, dragged off by sinister characters, raped even, yes, then tomorrow they'll find his body in the river! Call the police! We'll wait a bit longer, the father shot from his window. It's already after midnight, Dad!

So call then, go ahead, call.

Alphonse was still walking on a country road. It was night. The trees, on either side of the road, opened their arms to welcome him. Immersed in his story about Pierre-Paul-René, Alphonse was straining his imagination to extricate his hero from the most ludicrous of situations. It's quite a job to make up a story like this one! Alphonse said to himself.

Obviously, a child who doesn't come home one night, that's rather vague! What do you want us to do! We'll wait a bit, and tomorrow all the police stations in the capital will have all the particulars, and that's all we can do, and then we'll keep on waiting! People expect us to perform miracles! What's his name? Alphonse? Right, well... we'll see what we can do! My name is Victor, I'm the Police Inspector. Tomorrow I'll go do a little investigating to see what I can find out!

There was a picture of Alphonse on his desk and Victor looked at it distractedly. Victor is a really good policeman. Affable and understanding. Thank you. Alphonse. For once I'm not dealing with some hoodlum or scumbag.... Alphonse. Now all we have to do is find him.

Hello. I'm François, I live next door to Alphonse's family. I heard through the wall that Alphonse still hasn't come home! No, I don't sleep much at night. Alphonse, I know him a bit, we run into each other sometimes on the landing, in front of the elevator. We chat a bit. Hello Alphonse. Hi François! That sort of thing. Poor Alphonse! When they find him, they'll want to know why he left, they're going to ask for an explanation! Poor kid. As soon as you have to explain yourself things get complicated, because explaining yourself means justifying yourself, and justifying yourself is the end. Something's up, somewhere. The clues seem clear to me. Alphonse has disappeared. The whole world of the invisible is speaking to us through his disappearance. But no-one teaches us to tell the difference between lies and fiction.

GATHERING INFORMATION
AT ALPHONSE'S SCHOOL
——•——•——•——

Alphonse is quite a strange boy. A bit disturbed... yes, disturbed, in the clinical sense of the term of course! He's
the kind of pathological case I see quite often in my work
with young adolescents. Child psychology holds very few
surprises for an experienced clinician like myself. A boy has
disappeared. Well, we can understand his parents' anxiety,
but the desire to run away is simply a stage of adolescence.
Some kids do it, some don't, but all think about it at one
point or another. Isn't that right, my dear colleague?

Yes, yes, if you say so. Well, then I'll introduce myself, since we
have to introduce ourselves. I'm his French teacher,
Monsieur Gayaud. They just called me because I'm his
main teacher, that is, his homeroom teacher. Look, I have
no idea where Alphonse could be... and I don't care all
that much. You know, the teaching profession is very
demanding, you have to answer the students' questions,
know everything, and then there's the pressure from the
parents, and then whoops, a child just disappeared and *I*
get called! What do you want me to say? It all gets very
tiring. Alphonse! He's probably just getting into some mis-
chief with his friend, if you want my opinion.

The two men smoked their cigarettes in silence, then went
into the classroom where all the students were at their
desks. The principal was there, as well as the super-
intendent.

I'm Leon. I'm in Alphonse's class! Wait, I haven't finished–
—I'm Albert! I'm in Alphonse's class too (it's not just Leon!)
So they told us Alphonse disappeared, and they like want
to know what happened to him. Like, what we think and
all that. Wait, no wait, I'm not fini–
—I'm Arnold! *I'm* in Alphonse's class too! I told the principal,
and Monsieur Gayaud and the psychologist, I told them
what I thought of Alphonse. That I hadn't talked to him

that often, but that I didn't mind him as long as he didn't talk to me!

—Shut up Arnold! I'm Roger, the school jock. In sports everyone wants me on their team. Alphonse was kind of puny. But I like Alphonse. He was an ace at marbles, and I'm the same at sports so we had something in common! So my question is, Mr. Principal, is Alphonse dead?

"We don't think so. Your schoolmate has probably gotten lost. Which one of you knows him the best, or spent the most time with him? Jules turned around. I think Alphonse talked to Walter the most.

—And where is Walter?" the principal asked.

Monsieur Gayaud leaned over and told him that Walter hadn't come to school today because he was very sick.

"Well then! All we have to do is call Walter and we'll know where Alphonse is!" concluded the old Principal as he left the room.

WALTER, ALPHONSE'S FRIEND
———•———•———•———

Walter and Alphonse met one day. Nobody knows where or how. They say it happened very simply. Hi, I'm Walter. My name is Alphonse. And that was that. Walter gave Alphonse his cookies, and Alphonse won at marbles and shared his winnings with Walter.

Alphonse.... We didn't know where he came from. One day, just like that, I just saw him coming around the corner. His eyes were very gentle. He wasn't very good at grammar and when he didn't know how to answer, he would just look up and stare into space. I'm Walter; Alphonse used to be my best friend. I don't know what's happened since, but anyway... I still like Alphonse. Alphonse is so fantastic! He plays marbles and, you gotta admit, Alphonse is awesome at marbles! He could decimate *anyone* at marbles! But Alphonse doesn't like to argue, so if the other kids got too upset, not only did he never hesitate to give back all the marbles he'd won, he would smile and very discreetly slip in some of his own as well. Then he would always raise his head and gaze for a long time at the rooftops where every so often you could see people's laundry drying in the sun.

Before, when we were still talking to each other, we would meet in the morning to walk to school together. I would carry his bag and Alphonse, in a burst of morning enthusiasm, would launch into stories of his nocturnal adventures. His nocturnal adventures, give me a break.... He told me lies. He made me believe incredible things!! And I have to admit, I did believe him! For a long time I thought he was telling me the truth. Yeah, man, it was awesome! he would always start off.
Oh yeah? Let's hear!
And then he'd be off. And now that I'm telling you, I suspect he even made it up as he went along!
Guess what? he'd say. Last night, Walter, last night, an awesome thing happened. Three shady-looking guys were after

me, and I had to run all the way to the outskirts of the city
where they park the boats for the winter!

No way!

I swear to you, man! Yeah! I thought I was a goner. I swear,
I'm not stupid, you know, so I said to myself, Alphonse,
you gotta ditch them. So I climbed into a boat and there,
in the boats, there were all these sailors lying down – they
were sleeping! Then one woke up, he had tattoos up to his
eyeballs. The shady-looking guys got there and a fight
broke out. They were going at each other like you wouldn't
believe! I let them beat each other up and I took off and
so last night, I ended up sleeping in the subway!

No way!

And he would have bags under his eyes, so I believed him and
I would worry! He made me promise not to tell anyone!
He swore me to secrecy! And I believed him! I know now
that they were just stories he'd made up. But that's what he
was like. He'd lie awake all night so he could think up
incredible stories to tell me in the morning. I used to ask
him: Alphonse, what the hell gets into you wandering
around at night like that?

At night, Walter, there are lights that don't go out until the
first sign of daylight. They're just standing there in the
middle of the night. Windows of light. On the other side
of the light are things. People too, I guess. But you know,
Walter, people and things have never really interested me.
There were those lights, that was enough. It'll always be
enough. At night everything is so different: there isn't
enough light to see where the trees end. Everything merges
with the night: buildings, people, cranes and bulldozers you
can make out by the smell of their metal, they all climb
towards the night and embrace it, caress it. That's why
love, Walter, is especially at night. Yes, because everything
loses itself in us and we become bigger, more beautiful,
more generous with our bodies. At night, Walter, there's
only the orange moon that slips in slivers through the window grate and lingers softly over languorous bellies. The
night sculpts you, Walter. It's true, you can't see for miles
around the way you can in broad daylight, no, Walter – at
night, out of fear, you can only hold onto the things that

are right around you, and the darker the night, the more you see inside yourself, Walter, because you're really the only thing you can still see.

Walter, I love the night and the people who inhabit it. One day you'll come with me and you'll see.

Emmanuel Bilodeau in the Théâtre de l'Arrière-scène production.

Photograph by Jean-Guy Thibodeau.

VICTOR QUESTIONS ALPHONSE'S FAMILY
—————•————•————•————

Alphonse, like I said at the beginning, is my little brother!
   Sometimes, when my parents were asleep, we would hang
   out in the kitchen talking in whispers, and even though I
   had exams in the morning he would keep me up till three
   AM.
"My brother, do we have to experience different cultures to
   truly grasp the fact that we all only seek to be loved?"

Did he have a girlfriend? Victor asked.

You know, Inspector, we're a respectable family! My husband
   earns an honest living, and my son to whom you're refer-
   ring is a very intelligent boy! We're upstanding people, you
   know!

All right, all right Ma'am! We'll wait a while longer.

We've been waiting for three days! exclaimed the father
   who got up and left the room. The mother started crying
   again, moaning: What on earth could have gotten into
   Alphonse?! The brother remained standing, and the sister
   kept her head bowed, her hands in her lap. The sun, radi-
   ant and orange, gently lowered itself onto the smooth tiles
   of the kitchen floor. Victor got up and left the apartment.

They must be in an absolute panic at home, they must be
   worried half to death! That's what Alphonse was saying to
   himself as he walked along his country road when suddenly
   a phone started ringing. Pierre-Paul-René whirled around
   with a start and looked everywhere for some semblance of
   a telephone but there was nothing in sight. Not a leaf, not
   a stone, much less a telephone jack! Still, the ringing continued loud and clear. Confounded by the absurdity of the
   situation, he shouted just in case:
"Hello?
—Pierre-Paul-René?
—Speaking.

—Go north!
—Who is this?
—It's Flupan. Flupan-the-Evil-Flupan-the-glutton – Flupan!
—What do you want?

—Me? I don't want anything, my boy, I want the best for you,
     I'm telling you which way to go: Pastryburg is to the north.
—Why should I believe you? Huh?
—Because my goal is to lead you right into my clutches. I
     spend my time eating cookies and cakes, a little boy like
     you would make a succulent appetizer!
—Shut up!
—You see? You don't have a chance, you snotty-nosed brat, go
     back to your village, go away before I unleash my powers
     on you!!
—Go away!
—I can't go away because I'm not there!
—Hang up!
—I don't want to, I'm having too much fun!
—Then *I'm hanging* up. 'Click'."
Instant silence. Just the drone of the dial tone that soon gave
     way to a voice that insistently repeated: Please hang up and
     try your call again. Please hang up now…. Pierre-Paul-René
     continued on his way towards the north, towards the
     night. Soon, when darkness kneeled over the entire
     countryside, he could see a tiny glow, just above the
     horizon. It was the fortress of Pastryburg. The closer he
     got to his destination, the worse he slept at night because
     of horrible dreams in which a horrible Flupan used a cake
     recipe to turn him into popcorn. Not to mention the
     enticing smells of caramel custard, whipped cream and
     chocolate fudge that sometimes floated towards him from
     Pastryburg, teasing his nostrils.

THE PICTURE OF ALPHONSE IN THE NEWSPAPER (JUST A SMALL ONE)
———•———•———•———

For several days now, Alphonse's picture had been in the papers. (Just a small one, since the situation wasn't serious enough yet.)

Hello, I'm Judith. I just saw the picture. I wanted to introduce myself right away because soon—not right away, but soon—my name is undoubtedly going to come up. See you later.

VICTOR DOESN'T UNCOVER ANY NEW INFORMATION, BUT HE HEARS A STORY
———•———•———•———

Victor is a calm and thoughtful police inspector. On his way out of Alphonse's apartment he met François who was waiting for the elevator.

"Inspector, you have to understand. You're dealing with a dreamer.
—Yes, he's a child!
—He probably doesn't even know himself why he didn't come home, and now he can't turn back, since he knows full well that everyone's going to want to know what made him leave!
—True, said the Inspector. A young romantic.
—Listen, Inspector, I can't help you.
—So help me out then... you knew him well.
—Since you're asking my advice, I'll simply say that to find Alphonse, you have to search within the invisible.
—And what is this "invisible" you're always talking about? How do I access it?
—There might be something in this story, Mr. Inspector, that Alphonse told me one night when we ran into each other on the street. We walked home together taking our time, and Alphonse told me a story that he was incredibly excited about.
—What was it about?
—It was a story of a journey, about a strange man who went off on foot in search of a wild child. There was a mountain and a storm, I think.
—Tell it to me."

François couldn't remember all the details perfectly, but as the narrator, I don't want to repeat his hesitations since that will only slow things down. Here then is that famous story as it was told to François by Alphonse.

A man set off one fine morning along a country road that led to the foot of the mountain where, they said, a wild child who was a gentle boy with a one-note voice who was never surprised by anything lived among wolves in a cave near stretches of ice which at that altitude formed a plateau where ancient trees grew.

The sun rose weeping, and swept the fog off the road; the fog stretched and curled up, trying to snuggle even closer to the earth; the purple dawn glided towards the distant plains, and the night disappeared on the other side of the horizon. The opaque dampness completely swallowed the village; the mountain breeze blew gently, a storm was brewing.

When the man reached the foot of the mountain, he rested a moment on a huge boulder that jutted out from the roots of a tree. Clouds were slowly piling up on top of each other, making it so dark it was hard to see windows winking in the village nearby.

The man started off again. His climb lasted the whole morning and a good part of the afternoon; and, since he didn't have a watch and couldn't refer to the sun's position, he gradually completely lost his sense of reality thinking it was already far into the night while in fact, in the village where the fog was lifting, the clock of the church bells were only striking eight.

Since the paths were growing narrower and the mountainside steeper, the man had to make his way up by zigzagging! The sky was very low, and soon the man was lost in a cloud. It was only when he'd completely lost his sense of direction, could no longer tell if he was going up or down, and was gripped by the fear of falling or being attacked by an animal, mixed with a wild panic—that survival instinct that makes an animal tremble when it senses its death approaching—and was finally so tired and delirious he could no longer put one foot in front of the other, that he collapsed in the middle of the brambles and fell asleep. At that instant, the howling of wolves was heard...

François stopped his story for a moment. He took out a cigarette and offered one to Victor. They stayed like that for a long while, smoking in silence.

This won't help my investigation, but go on. It's so rare for someone to tell me a story in this damned line of work. Go on!

The man was awakened by the movement of the sky opening up. Bolts of lightening illuminated the horizon, relegating the day that was struggling to rise to twilight regions where it died at every clap of thunder. The wind played with the rain, darting and dancing with the drops in a crazy farandole, blowing bubbles of water into the air that briefly resembled a furtive shadow about to explode.

"Come on! Be strong!" the man said to himself. "It's only a storm. It will peter out eventually. And I'll get through it eventually. In two days it'll all be over. I just have to keep going, keep climbing higher and higher!"
He went on climbing. Here and there he grabbed onto whatever twigs he could, and when he glimpsed the dark mass of trees living higher up on the mountain, it gave him a second wind. But, at the curve of a little cloud the man saw the wolves for the first time. There were four of them, and they seemed to be waiting for him because as soon as he was facing them they moved towards him, lowering their heads as if in greeting, then turned and set off along the road, inviting him to follow. They led him higher, crossing through the clouds, winding 'round the rain, avoiding the wind, all the way to the summit of the storm from which they emerged to discover the firmament and the Milky Way spilling out along the sky. The wolves stationed themselves on a boulder that overlooked the valley and howled at the night. The man stood contemplating the cloudy mass of the storm: it formed a dark ocean at his feet and continued to unleash fierce torrents of rain.
It wasn't until the damp dawn that they arrived in front of a cave with a narrow opening. The wolves stood guard on either side of the entrance and lowered their heads once

again. The man squeezed through the narrow passage and pressed on until he could only continue by crawling! It was suddenly very cold. There was a smell of dead leaves that grew stronger where it was most damp. If the cave keeps narrowing I won't be able to go any further he said to himself. Sounds reached him from a distance, from the other side of the rocky walls. He crawled for a good while longer until he reached a cavity where he could almost stand up. Now look where I am! he sighed. Now I'm lost for good.

"I've been waiting for you for a long time."

The gentle wild child with a one-note voice who's never surprised by anything was there, beside him, in the bowels of the earth.

"You're here?

—I've been waiting for you for a long time!

—A long time? The man asked again.

—A long time! Yes!

—How old are you then, you whose voice is so old, so slow, and who people still call the 'wild child'?

—Like all children, my age varies according to the day. Sometimes I like to be as old as a tree.

—Can you see me?

—I can imagine you. It's nicer that way.

—Do you know where I come from, wild child, do you know what world I live in?

—Tell me.

—Listen. I come from a strange, lost world. Everything started one morning, when after getting up and walking outside, I saw that all those around me had a terrible despair in their eyes. All of them without exception, were walking and weeping as they walked. And crying out. I'd heard of you. So I came to see if your eyes contained the same terrible despair. But I can't see you. It's too dark!

—I'm a gentle child with a one-note voice and I'm never surprised by anything, since I'm not familiar with the world you describe.

—Does it make you unhappy, little child, not to know the world? Or does it make you happy?

—What do you think?

—It's hard to tell from your voice But it's possible that you're
no happier or unhappier than me.
—Then that doubt is more than enough. Don't you think?
Maybe that's what you call hope.
—You're awesome.
—I'm the wild child.
—Farewell.
—Farewell."
In the morning, some shepherds found him dead, frozen, at
the foot of the mountain. He was a man of about forty
whom no one could identify. Nobody knew him. Some had
seen him walk through the village the previous morning,
before the storm had struck the mountain.

Victor and François had been finished their cigarettes for a
while. Victor rose, and the two men shook hands.

It's a shame the man dies at the end, Victor said.
I shared that same thought with Alphonse. He said no, on the
contrary, it was better that way since the man had actually
died the moment he fell into the brambles, which meant
that the second part of the story, about the storm, the
wolves and the cave was his last dream. And a last dream,
in Alphonse's opinion, is a beautiful story to tell.

—A last dream! mused the Inspector.

VICTOR'S INVESTIGATION
CONTINUES AT SCHOOL AND IN THE
SURROUNDING AREA
—————•————•————•————

Tell me, Walter, what did you two do together when you didn't
    have school?
On Sundays, we used to go to the museum to laugh at the
    stuffed horses, Mr. Inspector.
And after that?
We also liked to run around in the big parks and it was always
    very late by the time we found our way home and said
    goodbye.
So you two got along very well it seems.
Well... Alphonse ate a lot of cookies. And I lost at marbles
    pretty much all the time. That was the secret of our
    friendship.

The children were gathered together in the sunlight of the
    schoolyard, sitting in a circle around Victor. It felt like one
    of those days at the end of the school year, when the sum-
    mer holidays are just around the corner, exams are over
    and the teachers, having nothing more to teach, just do fun
    activities with their students. But now, because Victor was
    so serious, the children weren't the least bit rowdy or
    unruly. Walter even had his head down and was having
    trouble hiding his immense sadness. Because Walter knew
    a thing or two about Alphonse.

We weren't too sure about Alphonse! In class, he always sat at
    the back and he never talked. All he did was smile!
It's true what Leopold says. Even the teacher was afraid of
    him! Plus, he was a liar!
Yeah, a big fat liar. I know. My name's Jules, and one day
    Alphonse tried to make me believe he was a secret agent
    hired by the government to spy on people his age in the
    schools! He tried to suck me in! But I'm not stupid!
I believed him a little. My name is Ahmed. One day I figured
    out that Alphonse was just telling stories! But me, Ahmed,

I said this to Alphonse and then, Alphonse, he didn't want to talk to me, Ahmed anymore.

Mr. Inspector! I'm the most serious one in the class, that is, the top student. You can ask Mr. Gayaud – he'll tell you "Hubert's the top student" – and I knew right away that all that talk about the night and sailors and everything was a bunch of lies. I told Walter and Walter could tell that Alphonse was just making up stories, so we all told Walter: "You have to watch Alphonse! He's a real weirdo! He isn't normal!" He tried to make us believe his mother was dead! He's a liar! He says all kinds of things, Mr. Policeman, all kinds of things! We don't even know where he comes from! And we told Walter: Alphonse is gonna fail, he's not a good student at all! You saw for yourself, at recess he sucks at sports and he whines his head off!

That's not true Walter replied. At marbles Alphonse is awe-some–

But we don't care about marbles, Walter, we don't give a shit, understand?

The Inspector took Walter aside and let his classmates go.

Does it upset you, what they say about Alphonse?

They're all jerks! Yesterday, when Alphonse had been missing for a week, they all acted like idiots!! They were saying the most horrible things about him – that he had choked to death on his own tongue, that he'd fallen off a bridge, and even worse stuff, but I know why Alphonse left, he was sick of it! Yeah, and now if he's dead, it's 'cause someone bashed his head in! Alphonse will always be at the foot of my bed. At night I hear him telling his fantastic stories, I see him in the mirror, sitting in the armchair, Alphonse is everywhere! He told me such beautiful stories, I believed every word! How can I be mad at him? For what? They were so beautiful!

When he reached the gates of Pastryburg, it was raining buck-ets. Entire clouds were bursting open one on top of the other. Pierre-Paul-René went up to two enormous wooden doors without any idea how he was going to go through them. They were adorned with heavy, solid gold sculptures and capped by a crown of ice. The keyhole was much too high and far too narrow. There was also an old man crouched in front of these doors, a hat pulled down over his eyes, and a beard that went on forever wrapped around him. Pierre-Paul-René stopped.

Who are you, boy?

Pierre-Paul-René.

Ahhh!!! So it's *you*.

Uh huh.

I'm warning you! If you don't answer my question correctly, I'll turn you into popcorn like all the others; if you give the right answer, I'll let you in and I'll grant you any two wishes you like.

Pierre-Paul-René looked around him and saw that he was ankle-deep in popcorn, and that from time to time, the old man would flick a piece into his mouth and crunch it.

So? Are you ready?

Yes.

Suddenly, a wild wind whipped itself around them, sending the popcorn whirling all over the place. The old man's hat hadn't moved at all, something that surprised even Pierre-Paul-René who is however a gentle boy with a one-note voice who's never surprised by anything. Night was starting to nibble away at the day. It was so strange! Pierre-Paul-René and the Old Man were standing there, at the threshold of night and the kingdom of dreams. The rain wouldn't stop, and the wind seemed to be rising from the earth. Then, as though he were reciting an incantation, the old man asked his question: "Why does a tree grow tall? Why does a man grow old? Why does a river run into the sea? Why does the earth keep turning? My question, Pierre-Paul-René, is the following: These four questions can be contained in a single question. What is that question?"

Still on the road, Alphonse found this sort of situation tricky because he himself—the one making up the story—didn't know the answer. He continued on his way, and pondered.

The imposing fortress facing Pierre-Paul-René seemed to be
looking at him tenderly. An owl landed for a moment on
the ramparts, hooting "hoo, hoo." The doors certainly
looked impenetrable, but he was sure they had a charming
side that would let anybody in.
The owl has found one of those sides; now it's up to me to find
another. Hoo... hoo... the owl disappeared. Pierre-Paul-
René then realized that everything was up to him, that he
could decide whether he was happy, worried, or even sad.
That he could, if he felt like it, be a good boy and go home
to his mother, who must be worried half to death. I don't
want to go back home. Then what do I want? To eat,
maybe. To sleep, to drink, to live! The day was starting to
make itself known. Since nature knows very well what it
wants, it doesn't fret or worry. Day exists because we need
day, the moon exists because it's beautiful. But me, I'm just
a kid, and I don't know how to do anything except keep
putting one foot in front of the other, why do I exist? Why
do I exist? he cried out loud, which made the old man start
and stagger towards him! Bravo, bravo, that's the correct
answer! Why do I exist? That's the right answer... now I'll
finally be able to shave! Quick my boy, what are your two
wishes?
"First of all, I'd like you to let my mother know I'm alright.
—Done.
—With no magic spell??
—You don't need a spell, because spells are only noise. Know,
young man, that a tree's branches and the peaks of mountains rise up in the silence of the invisible... and yet what
magic is greater than nature's? Abracadabras and other
hoopla are nothing more than circumstantial decorations
used by people who lack imagination. The man who makes
noise is a man who is frightened. Your second wish.
—I'd like to have all the recipes the evil Flupan took away with
him.
—Oh no! That would be too easy! Yes, too easy indeed! Pierre-
Paul-René, have you really thought about it? When you
return what will you tell all the children who are hungry
for details? What will you tell them? Children want
exciting adventures where danger is synonymous with

red roses! That's right! Pierre-Paul-René, if you manage to
recover the recipes yourself, and if you manage to get out
of Pastryburg alive, you'll become a hero that will inspire
future generations."

Pierre-Paul-René felt that the ultimate purpose of his mission
had just taken a different turn.
"Can I make another wish then?
—Yes.
—I'd like a kaleidoscope please, sir.
—You'll find one at the entrance to the city. And now, be off."
The doors yawned open slowly, so slowly that Pierre-Paul-René
had time to grow up and ponder. When the gap was wide
enough for him to slip through, Pierre-Paul-René stood up,
said goodbye to the old man, and squeezed through the
narrow opening.
That day, Pierre-Paul-René had just turned 14, but he didn't
know it.

The school bell rang. The children stood up and left the classroom, since the school day had just ended. As Walter was
leaving, he saw the Inspector come towards him. They
walked together, slowly, as they talked.
"So tell me, do you have any idea where he might have gone?

—Yes... well, no, not really, because I don't even know if that
person really exists or if it was just another one of his
stories!
—Who's that?
—A girl! He told me he was living a love story. Yes!
—What's her name?
—Judith. But it was only a story. I realize that now. What he
told me was just too crazy."

Wajdi Mouawad in the Théâtre de l'Arrière-scène production.

Photograph by Jean-Guy Thibodeau.

JUDITH

———•———•———•———

I introduced myself quickly a while ago, I'm Judith, so there
you go! It all started just like that. People thought it was a
love story. But generally, people believe anything. They saw
us walking hand in hand and rumours have been flying ever
since. In the holes in conversations, on street corners,
around cafés, on subway trains, on the radio and even in
the newspapers, all people talked about was the love that
had just blossomed between Alphonse and me.

Yes. I'm Judith. I'm one of the rare truths that Alphonse told
Walter, and the only one Walter didn't believe. You can't
really blame him, he was starting to distrust Alphonse.
That's partly why they stopped talking. Anyway...

How did the two of you meet?

Very simply, Inspector. Sitting on a bench, in the big park
downtown.

Hi, I'm Judith. He looked at me without a trace of surprise:
I'm Alphonse. And that was that. And then, slowly, things
started to happen very quickly. A look and then a smile...

Alphonse was still walking along a country road. At dawn he
had come across an old man.

Gotta bring in firewood for the winter!

Yes, sir.

Where are you going, boy?

Home, sir.

You're a good little boy.

Uh, sure.

And the old man continued on his way.

Alphonse so would have liked for someone to just take him by
the hand and tell him: this is how life is. That it's not
important to be successful at what you undertake, but
rather, to undertake what you'd like to succeed at. It
seemed to Alphonse that things were really backwards.
Yes, because of course when we meet those people, those
people who can comfort us, we meet them too late. They
always turn up when we're adults. You'd think there was a

conspiracy, Alphonse thought. When we become grown-ups we have furrowed eyebrows to show how terribly important we are (which is fine). But when we become grown-ups we don't want anyone to take us by the hand anymore, we wave our arms and we say, No! Out of my way! Let me by! Don't you see my furrowed eyebrows? Can't you see how busy I am?

After passing through the gates of the fortress, Pierre-Paul-René expected to find the city. But instead, there was a forest filled with a bizarre assortment of fruit trees. "I'm not there yet," he thought. The tree closest to him was an orange tree. Hanging from one of its branches was the kaleidoscope, which blended right in with the oranges. Pierre-Paul-René plucked it down. There was the woods. The forest was shamelessly cavorting with the horizon. Weird, he said. The wind suddenly encouraged him to enter the very quintessence of the forest. The sun was snuffed out and, with the forest so dense, Pierre-Paul-René found himself in utter, uncompromising blackness. He was afraid. Solitude had turned against him, the trees were suffocating him, the air was whistling in the dark and the darkness enveloped him in a bottomless night. The owls had disappeared, turning the forest's wisdom into a whirl-wind of cries, creaks and cracks that Pierre-Paul-René's imagination was magnifying into all sorts of monstrosities. At dawn, the dampness hammering at him, he collapsed at the mouth of a cave, convinced he'd be devoured by the monsters of his mind.

The fog rose and so did Alphonse. He kissed me on the lips and said "Goodbye, Judith. Thank you." He handed me a letter and he left. That was the last day anyone saw him.

Can you read me that letter, Miss?
Of course, but you mustn't talk about it. It's better for his parents to believe I'm a lie.
Here is that letter:

Judith,

It's no secret, this is Alphonse writing to Judith. I'm sitting down in an armchair and I'm writing to you. Because I love you very much. This isn't a declaration of love.

Judith, I'm afraid. Because I don't think life will bring us any closer together. I'm writing to you and you aren't answering me, I'm writing to you and you don't know that I'm writing to you. Do you ever think about me? Judith, I'm not happy here where I am, I'm not happy!

I've come to tell you who I am. It isn't easy because I'm young, and at my age you aren't supposed to say such things. I love you, but I'm afraid. I don't want to scare you, frighten you, see you run the way wild horses run. I love you.

How to tell you who I am? My name is Alphonse but that's just a convention.

What I love about you isn't your face, because your face isn't you, but something that belongs to you. Just like your smile, your legs and your hands, which are part of you, but not the essence of you. You're much more than a hand or a face and it's you that I love Judith.

Close your eyes. Listen. Listen to the rain on my face. Listen. You told me yesterday your name was Judith. Come. There's a cliff, a cliff, where it's good to jump, where it's good to die. I wish the storm would make three times as much racket.

Come on! A simple leap! Then we'd see life from a bit higher up, we'll fly like migratory birds. I'll show you fragile places, you'll learn to weep the way eagles weep when they fall beneath the storm, come, we'll fly away and we'll see the oceans, we'll see them flow into each other, their blues, their reds, we'll see the oceans make love to each other to give birth to new continents, come with me, let's return to that special cliff. Come. You'll know who I am.

Alphonse

Judith?
Yes, Mr. Inspector?
Where could he be?
I don't know, Mr. Inspector.

Alphonse was still walking straight ahead, determined to
follow the road that would lead him north. But since
Alphonse had no sense of direction and since he didn't
realize he had no sense of direction, he had no idea he was
actually walking west, and that if he continued that way
he'd be completely lost, and that in fact he was a bit lost
already. A car pulls up beside him. The window rolls down.
Where are you going, lad? Home. Right. And where might
your home be? My home? ...ummm... (Alphonse gestured
vaguely) That way! And guess which way the police station
is! Let's go! In the car, laddie! Everyone's been looking for
you for the past two weeks!
Now Pierre-Paul-René is lying in the belly of the cave. Being a
hero to inspire future generations doesn't interest me any
more. The complex architecture of the cave was weighing
on his feelings. Not far from him, a stalactite was dripping.
Each drop would appear, detach itself slowly, break away
from the stone, hang in the air for a moment, then crash
onto the rock an instant later.
Why are you weeping, cave?
There is the known and the unknown.

Pierre-Paul-René didn't dare to ask any other questions.

I am the cave. I'm the open mouth of mountains and I shelter
beings from the rain. And for centuries I've been weeping
because I'm growing old, and I weep because I'm growing
weak! So much weight rests on me. So I weep and my tears
climb, they climb, and, becoming solid, they rise to my
ceiling to help me support all that weight; but a day will
come when all these columns of tears will fill me. And then
I'll disappear.
You weep so you can disappear, cave? That isn't a good idea.
I weep to change.
There must be other ways to change, cave.

This is the only way I know. I'm only a cave.

A while ago, there were monsters who wanted to devour my chest. It hurt so much I wept too.

Changing isn't easy. Ideas, beautiful things change; they know how to change, because to change is to go beyond pain, to change is to disappear one day and then fill the space with yourself! That's the great secret of caves.

AT THE POLICE STATION
——•——•——•——

When I saw him come in, he looked like every kid who's
brought into the police station after being caught. Eyes
downcast and worried. They're all like that in the face of
power. In the face of authority. But if he only knew how
endearing I found him, maybe then he'd have smiled at me.
We get so many scumbags parading through here all day
long, a boy like Alphonse is a real gem. I'm Victor, the
Inspector for the police station. I think I already told you
that. Anyway, Alphonse wouldn't look at me. I was happy
to know his parents lived so far away, it'd take them a while
to come and get him. An hour, maybe. An hour to get him
to look at me.

The sister, in her bed, started to cry. Alphonse is coming
home, I'll be able to sleep. My mother, in the living room,
still hasn't spoken a word to my father who must be waiting by the window as usual, a cigarette in his heartstrings.
My other brother has left to get Alphonse at the police
station. I'd like to leave too! Go off towards the midnight
sun and freeze to death...
She closed her eyes.
Alphonse opened his.
His brother was there, standing beside Victor.
His brother signed the release forms and I watched them
leave. I never saw Alphonse again, but they say he's happy
now, in some other country.

THE RIDE HOME AND MEMORIES
OF DRIVES PAST
————•———•———•————

It was a long drive. Alphonse's forehead was pressed against
the rear window of the taxi. A very long time ago, when
Alphonse was still small, every Sunday the whole family
would go for a drive.

In the car, they would sleep. It was quiet, it was boring, and it
was carefree. They rarely remembered their dreams.
Maybe the car was moving too fast, there's no time to fig-
ure things out, get oriented. The mountains in the distance
were touching down on the earth, clouds were clinging to
them. When Alphonse's father drove, no one could tell
what was going through his head. But the signs seemed
reassuring. A smile, he turned on the radio... he was trying
not to worry, today was Sunday.... As for the rain, it
spawned more drops on the rear window; on Sundays,
when the father took the whole family to a restaurant
overlooking a ravine, the sun was often hanging out
somewhere behind the rain. The rain too was part of
the Sunday ritual.

Alphonse didn't like sitting in the middle of the back seat
between his brother on the right and his sister on the left.
You couldn't sleep there. You couldn't see into the ravines
and you couldn't see the seashore. It was the most insignif-
icant place to sit, and they put him there just because he
was the smallest. No one ever seemed to notice these sorts
of injustices.

On lonely roads, where no other cars kept them company,
roads that wound endlessly above ravines, roads from
which the city appeared at their feet even dirtier than
before, it seemed to Alphonse that they were alone in the
world. At those moments the radio would inevitably be
playing a slow song, with long monotonous chants, a song
where a single voice recounted the tragic epic of some
Persian king. At those moments, everyone was silent. His
sister, brother and mother would look out their respective
windows; only his father, smiling, would still be staring

straight ahead. The wonderful road, twisting and turning, surrounded by cedars and pines with their arms wide open, showed him the path to happiness.

"So, Alphonse," his father would ask, "Are you hungry?"

Sometimes we respond awkwardly to those affectionate questions, and then we think that all is ruined. Things really changed. Yes. His father wasn't sad and unhappy yet, wasn't making compromises, he was trying to be happy. Those drives every Sunday were a recipe for happiness that, years later, proved not to be enough.

Pierre-Paul-René now finds himself in the most hidden, the most intimate, most secret place in the cave. There is rock all around his hunched body and there is a terrible rumbling.

Cave! I'm afraid of this rumbling I hear.

What you hear, boy, is the sound of the universe moving forward, over there, on the other side of the invisible! This sound, the origin of all life, can only be heard in the depths of caves. Listen to it; let it cradle you; let it lull you to sleep, I am the cave! Here, nothing can hurt you!

What some of us have to go through for a little chocolate cake, thought Pierre-Paul-René.

Desserts had always posed a problem. The choice was never made without a few tears, and very often Alphonse lost all appetite, to the great delight of his brother who'd get to eat the dessert their mother would end up choosing.

We always sat at the same table, in the same places, just like at home during the week; even in the restaurant the family wore the same faces as usual. For Alphonse, the setting didn't break the phenomenal silence of his childhood.

Obviously, the drive home was more tedious. It was nighttime, with the whiff of "enough fun and games" floating in the air. The father seemed preoccupied by business at the office, he was no longer smiling, and the sense of the invisible had disappeared.

Pierre-Paul-René, still lying in the belly of the cave, had a dream. He dreamed about Alphonse, walking along his

country road. He saw him climb up a tree and turn
  towards him.
Hello Pierre-Paul-René.
Hello Alphonse.
Recite me a poem, Pierre-Paul-René.
I'll never reach Flupan's castle, Alphonse.
Recite me a poem, then open your eyes and you'll see.
A poem, Alphonse? ...All right.
Poem.
We have only one candle left to recognize the world that
  surrounds us.
We mustn't hide anymore.
Look ahead.
Where is life? It's so often somewhere else.
Beyond our disasters of the heart, we will remain true to each
  other.
How can I forget you without killing you?
And I'd a thousand times rather kill you than leave you behind
  on the threshold of my memory.
My friendship for you is so strong that in spite of you, I'll
  remain your strength. Your friendship is so clear that
  I need only say the word to begin the journey.

The boy you call Alphonse doesn't seem to be feeling too hot,
  eh... I'm the taxi driver who drove him home from the
  police station. His brother sat beside me and yakked about
  the weather the whole time... what it was like today, what
  it would be like tomorrow and after that.... It's strange –
  now that I'm telling you all this, something just came back
  to me. At one point in the night sky there was an amazingly bright lightning bolt and it started to rain.

What the taxi driver didn't know, and what I'm going to tell
  you, is that the amazingly bright lightning bolt was Pierre-
  Paul-René entering Flupan's castle. When he opened his
  eyes, he found himself sitting in the taxi on the back seat
  beside Alphonse, but neither the taxi driver, nor Alphonse's
  brother had noticed a thing. Alphonse and Pierre-Paul-
  René, who were pressed up against each other, whispered
  in each other's ears so they wouldn't be overheard.

"Hi, Alphonse.

—Hi, Pierre-Paul-René.

—I recited the poem, there was an incredible light and I was inside Flupan's castle.

—You see Pierre-Paul-René? Flupan's castle is the world I live in. Flupan's castle is the school and the traffic lights and the sidewalks and the buildings and the mountains and this taxi and this taxi driver – all of this is Flupan's castle.

—The recipes could be hidden anywhere.

—Yes, Pierre-Paul-René, anywhere at all.

—Oh well. Listen, Alphonse, I promised to bring back those recipes, so I'll have to keep on looking.

—Wait, Pierre-Paul-René, I'll never be able to survive here, in this world. You stay here and I'll go back to your world, where the brontosauri frolic on the grass and the vacuum cleaners speak and are kings.

—You'll comfort my mother for me, answered Pierre-Paul-René.

—And you'll do the same for mine, said Alphonse."

And Alphonse and Pierre-Paul-René, who looked so much alike, parted ways once again. In a splendid flash of lightning, Alphonse went back to Pierre-Paul-René's world, and Pierre-Paul-René remained behind in the taxi.

And, coincidentally, the taxi had just come to a stop in front of Alphonse's apartment building.

ALPHONSE

———•———•———•———

I am Alphonse.

I'm the one people have said all kinds of things about from the
beginning. I didn't mean to run away, or escape, I wasn't
sad or unhappy and I loved my parents very much... in fact
what happened is much simpler. I simply went in the
wrong direction taking the subway home after school.
I didn't get off at the next station. Too tired. So I kept
going, right to the end of the line. Everybody knows that
in certain situations we don't know how to react. And
when the invisible opens before us, it's terrifying. No one
teaches us anything about the invisible. Not a thing. When
we're children, no one tells us much. For example, when
I was small, no one ever told me that the Earth is in a
galaxy and that the stars are formed from a pile of star dust
that binds together and forms a mass and grows and grows
till it collapses onto itself and dying, creates enough energy
to shine, sometimes for millions of years. No one ever said
a word to me about that. But had I known, it seems to me
that yes, it would have comforted me! Yes, it would have
helped me sleep.

When Pierre-Paul-René entered the apartment, I don't know
exactly what happened. But I can easily imagine. The front
door. The hallway, my mother in the living room knitting,
my father not talking, my sister sleeping (she must have
been pretending) and my brother walking behind Pierre-
Paul-René, all the way to my bed. Pierre-Paul-René lay
down, he slept. That must be how things went; but what
I'm sure of, is that no one noticed a thing. No one could
tell the difference between Pierre-Paul-René and me. And
no one will ever see the difference, because no one believes
in Pierre-Paul-René. Everyone thinks that Pierre-Paul-
René doesn't exist, people think that Pierre-Paul-René is a
figment of my imagination! So they smile and look at each
other and say: Oh, that Alphonse! Honestly! What an
imagination! People only believe in what they can see and
touch! In fact, people don't want to believe anymore! They

want to know. They don't *believe* that the earth is round, they know it. They don't *believe* that the sky is blue, they know it! And people have trapped what they know about me. What they knew about me. But the rest, everything else that's inside me, and around me, and that belongs to me, that part of me that's so small it has to be *believed in*, that part that's even more real than my flesh and blood can ever be, that part that their tired eyes will never be able to see, they haven't caught that part of me, it's still on the road as free as the colours of the night. That part of me is hidden, tucked away, buried; *that's* the part of me that *truly exists*. At least I want to believe that... I want to believe it, so that life, which is just beginning for me, and death, which could strike me at any moment, will both be easier to accept, more joyful, and more beautiful.

Wajdi Mouawad
in the Théâtre de
l'Arrière-scène
production.

Photograph by
Jean-Guy
Thibodeau.

TRANSLATOR

Shelley Tepperman is a Toronto-born, Montreal-based dramaturg and translator with special interests in new play development and translation dramaturgy. She translates from French, Spanish and Italian, and has translated more than twenty-five plays for stage and radio. She has worked with theatres across the country, as well as with the Canadian Broadcasting Corporation, where she has been involved in developing and producing radio drama. She also writes for documentary television. This is her fifth collaboration with Wajdi Mouawad.

PLAYWRIGHT

Wajdi Mouawad is Lebanese in his childhood, French in his way of thinking and Québécois in his theatre. That's what happens when you spend your childhood in Beirut, your adolescence in Paris and then try to become an adult in Montreal.

Since graduating from the National Theatre School of Canada Wajdi Mouawad has written, adapted, translated and directed stage plays for audiences of all ages. He also founded the Théâtre Ô Parleur with Isabelle Leblanc, to celebrate language and ideas and send them travelling.

If Wajdi Mouawad had a punching bag he wouldn't write anymore.

Since January 2000, Wajdi Mouawad has been at the helm of Montreal's Théâtre de Quat'Sous. He has been programming seasons that voyage through the words of the shipwrecked.

Works published by Lémeac-Actes Sud: *Pacamambo, Rêves, Littoral, Les Mains d'Edwige au moment de la naissance, Alphonse.* In English translation: *Wedding Day at the Cro-magnons, Tideline, Alphonse* (Playwrights Canada Press).

—Estelle Savasta